IMAGES
of Rail

TENNESSEE CENTRAL RAILWAY
THE FIRST 50 YEARS

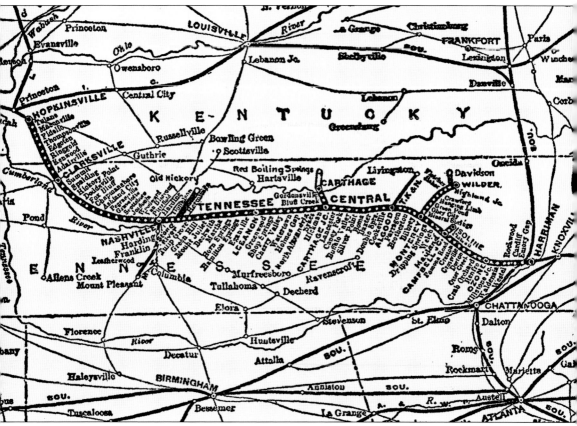

The map depicts the 296-mile Tennessee Central Railway (TC) at its zenith during the 1920s, showing the main line and branches to Old Hickory, Carthage, Wilder, and Isoline. During the Great Depression, the TC's mileage decreased dramatically with the abandonment of unprofitable branch lines and spurs. (Author's collection.)

IMAGES
of Rail

TENNESSEE CENTRAL RAILWAY
THE FIRST 50 YEARS

Ralcon Wagner

ARCADIA
PUBLISHING

Published by Arcadia Publishing
Charleston, South Carolina

Printed in the United States of America

Library of Congress Control Number: 2022944861

For all general information, please contact Arcadia Publishing:
Telephone 843-853-2070
Fax 843-853-0044
E-mail sales@arcadiapublishing.com
For customer service and orders:
Toll-Free 1-888-313-2665

Visit us on the Internet at www.arcadiapublishing.com

*In memory of Virgil King (1939–2021),
a Tennessee Central Railway employee, historian, and friend.
Virgil would have loved to have written this book!*

Contents

ACKNOWLEDGMENTS

For any project to be successful, there is always a group of dedicated and talented people with a passion for keeping history alive and who are instrumental in helping to put all the pieces together. The author gratefully acknowledges the many folks who helped to bring this history to printed form.

First and foremost, my gratitude goes out to the professional staff at the Metro Nashville Archives, Tennessee State Library & Archives, and also the Center for Railroad Photography & Art, for sharing the many vintage photographs and information needed to document the history of the Tennessee Central Railway.

Equally important was the support from Charles Buccola and Amy Hanaford Purcell of the Archives & Special Collections at the University of Louisville, Nick Fry of the John W. Barriger III National Railroad Library, the St. Louis Mercantile Library, George R. Zepp of Historic Rugby Inc., Dale Welch of the Monterey Depot Museum, the Wilson County Archives, and the Cumberland County Archives & Family Heritage Center.

Special thanks to James D. Le Croy, G. Battle Claiborne, Dr. W.O. Greene III, Dr. John Payne, Bob Bell Jr., and Robert Thurman for generously sharing images from their personal collections. I also wish to recognize local history scholar Dr. Carole Bucy as well and Allen Forkum, editor of the *Nashville Retrospect*, for their inspiration and for encouraging me to write this book.

The author wishes to express his gratitude to Stacia Bannerman, title manager at Arcadia Publishing, for her continued encouragement.

Very importantly, thanks to Gene Hawkins for his assistance with choosing images, providing guidance with page layouts, and fact-checking the text.

And special thanks to my wife, Rita, for her continued patience and willingness to assist with proofing the copy and providing new ideas.

INTRODUCTION

The Tennessee Central Railway was originally conceived during the 1880s as a coal-hauling line. The intention was to haul coal and other minerals from mines in Fentress and Roane Counties to the Cincinnati Southern Railroad at Harriman. In later years, coal hauling proved to be less profitable than expected, so the TC pushed westward, reaching Nashville in 1902. Soon, the railroad was extended farther northwest, ultimately reaching Hopkinsville, Kentucky, in late 1903. The expansion was a wise decision; the types of goods hauled by the TC were now more diverse. Here, the TC interchanged with the Illinois Central Railroad, providing an important link to northern and eastern markets and an alternative route to the rival Louisville & Nashville Railroad.

While the TC represented a small portion of the nation's rail network, the 296-mile class-one railroad was a vital link to the region it serves. For the towns between Nashville and Knoxville, it was the only practical means of transportation to the outside world before the era of paved roads. It was how people had their mail delivered, received packages, and most importantly, visited friends and family in distant locations.

People living along the TC truly felt like it was *their* railroad. Most everyone, especially in the small communities, knew at least one person employed with the company—whether it was an agent at the depot, train conductor, or engineer. In some cases, these folks were also relatives. The track between Carthage Junction and Harriman traversed some of the most rugged terrain in middle Tennessee, passing through towns with names such as Buffalo Valley, Sebowisha, Otter Creek, Crab Orchard, and Emory Gap.

During its first years of operation, the TC referred to itself as "the Sunrise Route." Over the next several years, the official slogan changed to "the Nashville Route." From the beginning, railroad employees were very personal and attentive to the needs of both shippers and passengers in all the towns they served. To reflect this, TC management soon changed its slogan again to "The Road of Personal Service."

The railroad was made up of two divisions. The Eastern Division, everything east of Nashville to Harriman, included the branches to Old Hickory, Carthage, Crawford, and Isoline. The Western Division included the track west of Nashville to Clarksville and Hopkinsville. Each division had its own unique characteristics. The Eastern Division had the steepest grades and biggest operational challenges for the railroad. Until the early 1940s, it produced the most revenue for the TC; the region between Monterey and Harriman was the location of numerous coal mines and heavy industry. On the other hand, the Western Division, while still vital to the railroad as a connection to the Illinois Central at Hopkinsville, had substantially less traffic and fewer shippers. The exception to this was Clarksville, the second largest city on the TC after Nashville, which served several customers.

Over the years, the length of the TC changed a couple of times after the entire system was initially completed in 1904. The railroad gained eight miles after acquiring an eight-mile track from the US government that had formerly served a gunpowder plant constructed during

World War I. The line was quickly constructed in 1918 linking the plant at Old Hickory to a connection with both the Nashville, Chattanooga & St. Louis Railway (NC&StL) and the TC at Stone River Junction. The NC&StL was contracted by the government to operate most of the freight trains bringing supplies to the factory. A short-lived commuter train service also operated over the route to bring defense workers in from Nashville. The TC supplied freight trains over the line as well in support of the war effort. But in November 1918, the war was over. The government quickly closed the gunpowder plant, idling its railroad track. A few years later, the line was put up for sale and offered to the NC&StL, which turned it down. After it was offered to the TC, the railroad purchased it from the government in 1923. The new acquisition became the Old Hickory branch.

The Isoline branch was originally incorporated as the Cumberland Plateau Railroad in 1901. It was absorbed by the TC the following year. The eight-mile branch connecting to the TC's main track at Campbell Junction was built to serve the mines of the Clear Creek Coal Company. Around 1920, the company shut down after most of its coal was depleted. All traffic on the branch disappeared, and it was dormant for many years. The Isolene branch was officially abandoned in 1939. This would be the last major abandonment of a TC branch line. However, in 1959, a short spur track on the Crawford branch between Highland Junction and Davidson was abandoned, also attributed to a mine closure.

During much of its 75-year roller-coaster history, the TC struggled to survive amid financial setbacks and increasing debt. Over the years, the railroad was able to make several purchases of locomotives and equipment to improve service as business increased, including acquiring new engines in 1902. The company acquired secondhand former New York Central Railroad Mikado-type locomotives during the late 1930s and early 1940s. Around this same time, the Mikados were joined by secondhand Norfolk & Western Railway articulated engines to meet the TC's need for heavier and more powerful locomotives.

Due to the numerous sharp curves and steep grades on the TC, passenger trains could only travel at a maximum of 40 miles per hour on the fastest portions of the railroad; 30 miles per hour was the fastest speed for freight trains. Movements of trains are controlled by timetables, train orders, and manual block signals across the entire railroad. While TC's passenger trains were not particularly fast, these "accommodations" were punctual as a rule. Trains typically consisted of a railway post office car, baggage-express car, and two coaches and made stops wherever passengers wanted to board or disembark—even if not a scheduled stop on the timetable.

In December 1939, the TC dedicated its first diesel locomotive, No. 50. Built by the American Locomotive Company (ALCO), the unit was placed on display near the Nashville passenger depot where city leaders and railroad officials posed for photographs. The diesel locomotive was purchased in response to the city's continuing problems with dirty air caused by coal smoke. This switch engine was primarily used to switch cars at Nashville's yard and various industries in the area.

Beginning in the late 1940s and continuing through the 1950s, the railroad purchased several diesel road switchers from ALCO. Four of these units, along with 200 new hopper cars, were financed with a loan from the Reconstruction Finance Corporation in 1952. This latter equipment acquisition helped the TC handle the anticipated growth in traffic generated by the opening of the Kingston Steam Plant the following year.

Throughout the decades, TC's management genuinely cared about its employees and their families, doing everything they could to promote a family-like environment on the job. Each summer the company held a picnic, encouraging everyone to attend. During the mid-1950s, at the suggestion of several employees, the TC started publishing its own company magazine, *The Highballer*. The purpose was to recognize employees and their families. It also covered the latest company news, such as the purchase of new locomotives and rolling stock, or new industries along the line. While very popular with employees, the TC suddenly ceased publication of the magazine two years later for unknown reasons.

By the mid-1950s, a new threat was looming for the TC. Decades earlier, rival Louisville & Nashville Railroad did whatever it could to stop the expansion of the TC during the 1890s through

1905. The railroad was now facing its biggest challenge yet. Since the 1930s, a federal plan to build a network of superhighways had been proposed but never successfully funded. In the mid-1950s, the National Interstate and Defense Highways Act was created. This authorized the building of highways throughout the country, which would be the biggest public works project in the nation's history. The highway designated as Interstate 40 would cross the length of Tennessee by way of Memphis, Nashville, and Knoxville. Of most concern to TC management was that the path of Interstate 40 closely paralleled most of the railroad's Eastern Division between Nashville and Harriman. This included most of the intermediate cities served by the TC. The new interstate highway would create a large advantage for the trucking industry.

In the years to come, the TC faced new challenges as it struggled to pay off its loan to the Reconstruction Finance Corporation while experiencing serious declines in business and revenue.

For brevity, the Tennessee Central Railway will be referred to as "TC" throughout the book. All cities and communities mentioned are in Tennessee unless specified otherwise.

Every effort has been made to correctly identify individuals and locations in photographs and to provide accurate information throughout this book. However, some names and information have been lost to history. This is not intended to be a detailed history of the railroad, but one covering the company's highlights, as well as a visual record of images from approximately 1900 to the mid-1950s.

The Tennessee Central Railway's logo is instantly recognizable to anyone who had business with the railroad or rode its passenger trains. The intertwined "T" and "C" inside a circle was a simple but effective herald that identified the company's brand to everyone in the region it served. The design dates to 1902 or perhaps earlier. The logo adorned virtually everything connected to the TC. This included advertisements, timetables, official correspondence, and even many diesel locomotives. Over the years, the appearance varied when the typeface was simplified, giving the railroad a more modern image in later years. (Author's collection.)

One

COL. JERE BAXTER, VISIONARY

Col. Jeremiah "Jere" Baxter accomplished more in his lifetime than most of his contemporaries. Many described him as a "steam engine on legs." Baxter never really got the full respect he deserved for his many accomplishments. While he was often referred to as the "father of the Tennessee Central," the colonel was not initially involved with building the railroad that would become the TC. It was later in life that he invested in and promoted the railroad. Baxter, born in Tennessee in 1852, was the son of a prominent Nashville judge. After attending school in Nashville, he studied law and soon started traveling, looking for new business opportunities. At an early age, he obtained a controlling interest in the Memphis & Charleston Railroad, later becoming its president. Baxter soon became a promoter of and investor in coal mines in Alabama. It was around 1893 that he began to promote his idea of a railroad that joined Nashville with East Tennessee, calling it the Tennessee Central. He felt that railroads such as Louisville & Nashville (L&N) and Nashville, Chattanooga & St. Louis had a monopoly on Nashville, but also felt that an east-west route was needed to connect with Knoxville. Baxter decided to ask the people of Nashville, through their city government, to invest a million dollars in his proposed railroad. After much debate, a city-wide referendum was held. The citizens voted in favor of Baxter's proposition to subsidize his new line. Not surprisingly, the L&N and NC&StL opposed Baxter's proposal and secured a court injunction against it. In desperation, Baxter used his personal money, ultimately traveling to St. Louis for additional investors to secure needed capital. He successfully found the funding to build the TC. In May 1902, the first TC train arrived in Nashville full of dignitaries. Baxter died on February 29, 1904, at 52 years old. He was interred at Nashville's Mount Olivet Cemetery. Ironically, his grave is unmarked, and its precise location is unknown. This seems a cruel snub to a great man who left such an indelible mark on his city and his state.

Col. Jere Baxter was a man of many talents—attorney, businessman, newspaper publisher, philanthropist, and also founder and financier of the Tennessee Central Railway. He was born in Tennessee in 1852. He graduated from Montgomery Bell Academy and later studied law. During his political career, he served in the Tennessee state senate and ran unsuccessfully for governor in 1890. (Tennessee State Library & Archives.)

Attorney and circuit court judge Nathanial Baxter Sr., at left, poses for a formal portrait with his three sons, from left to right, Tennessee house speaker Nathanial Baxter Jr., Edmund Baxter, and Jere Baxter in Nashville around 1890. The Baxter family was involved with Tennessee politics and business for decades throughout the 19th century. During the Civil War, Judge Baxter sympathized with the Union, but his four sons fought for the Confederate army. The youngest son, Jones Fletcher Baxter, was killed in a gunfight in 1878. Although Jere is the youngest brother in the photograph, he also died very young, at the age of 52 in 1904. (Tennessee State Library & Archives.)

When Colonel Baxter died suddenly in 1904, Tennesseans were saddened by the loss. Later that year, $10,000 was raised for the construction of a monument to his memory. The statue, dedicated on May 26, 1907, was initially displayed at Broadway and Sixteenth Avenue in Nashville. Since then, it has been relocated several miles across town. Today, the monument is in front of Jere Baxter Middle School near the East Nashville community. (Author photograph.)

Two

THE EARLY DAYS

The early history of the TC—between 1893 and 1922—has always been confusing to follow for both researchers and railroad history buffs. Because of various bankruptcies and reorganizations, the name switched back and forth several times over the course of 29 years, from Tennessee Central Railroad to Tennessee Central Railway, to differentiate each newly-chartered company from the previous one that had failed. Col. Jere Baxter chartered the original Tennessee Central Railroad in 1893. He had long aspired to build a railroad to connect eastern lines with the existing Nashville & Knoxville Railroad (N&K) at Monterey, creating a continuous line to Lebanon, 32 miles east of Nashville. The N&K was financed and chartered by Alexander Crawford of Pennsylvania in 1884. An existing railroad, the Nashville, Chattanooga & St. Louis Railway, already connected Nashville with the N&K in Lebanon. Baxter soon had financial problems after a contractor working for him went bankrupt and was unable to continue work on the right-of-way. Baxter lost control of his railroad. A few years later, he raised the necessary funds from investors to buy back the railroad when it was sold off. Baxter soon completed the unfinished portion of the track between Monterey and Emory Gap. In 1902, the Tennessee Central Railway was sold to the Tennessee Central Railroad Company. The new corporation wasted no time in acquiring smaller railroads in the mid-state area, including the Cumberland Plateau Railroad, the Nashville & Clarksville Railroad, and the aforementioned Nashville & Knoxville. In May of that year, a group of dignitaries including Colonel Baxter rode the first train to Nashville from Lebanon over the newly opened track, allowing passengers to travel to the eastern part of the state without changing trains. The following year, the TC was extended west to Ashland City. The line reached its western terminus of Hopkinsville in 1904. Later that year, after seeing the completion of his railroad, Baxter died suddenly at the age of 52.

Above, work is progressing on a portion of the Tennessee Central Railway at an unidentified location in Cumberland County as construction workers pose next to their steam shovel. In the image below, taken in the same area, rock and dirt are loaded onto gondolas to clear the right-of-way. These views are from around 1900. (Both, Tennessee State Library & Archives.)

A major challenge when building the TC was the construction of numerous trestles required along the line, but none was more impressive than the Piney Creek Bridge near Westel. The massive structure was arguably the tallest on the railroad and an engineering marvel at the time it was built. (Louisville & Nashville Railroad Company Records, University Archives and Records Center, University of Louisville.)

The Millstone Creek Bridge, about a mile east of Ozone, is one of the numerous bridges spread across TC's system. This timber structure had just been built when this photograph was taken around 1901. Over the years, however, it was surely a continued source of maintenance issues for the division superintendent. (Louisville & Nashville Railroad Company Records, University Archives and Records Center, University of Louisville.)

When railroads were being built, the contractor furnished its employees with food and shelter at the construction site utilizing a work train. This consisted of several sleeping cars, a kitchen car, and one for storing tools and equipment. This arrangement maximized efficiency for both the crew and the contractor. This image was captured at an unknown location on the TC. (Tennessee State Library & Archives.)

The citizens of Crossville turned out in force to see TC's first train arrive in their city in 1895. The newly-built segment, financed by Jere Baxter, extended the former Nashville & Knoxville Railroad 55 miles east to Emory Gap, ultimately becoming an important part of the railroad's Eastern Division between Nashville and Harriman. (Tennessee State Library & Archives.)

It was a great day of celebration as a group of dignitaries and railroad officials pose in front of TC's first train on May 24, 1902, in Nashville. The event was front-page news in papers across the state. The new route allowed people from middle Tennessee to travel by train to Knoxville and other points in the eastern part of the state without having to travel to Chattanooga to make connections. Below, commemorative ribbons were given out to participants to mark the special occasion. (Both, Historic Rugby Archives.)

FIRST TRAIN

Tennessee Central R.R.

NASHVILLE MAY 27, 1902

The early passenger timetables issued by the TC in 1902 featured attractive artwork, details about the company, and a map of the railroad, as well as schedules and accommodations for all trains. In those early days, the railroad referred to itself as "the Sunrise Route" and featured named passenger trains such as the Volunteer State Limited, Nashville Day Express, and "the Shopping Train." After a few years, these names were dropped. By the early 1920s, many trains were discontinued due to improved highways and declining ridership, leaving two trains on the Eastern Division. (Historic Rugby Archives.)

SUNRISE ROUTE VIA HARRIMAN, TENN.

TENNESSEE CENTRAL RAILROAD COMPANY

NASHVILLE

JERE. BAXTER,
PRESIDENT.

G. A. CLARK,
GEN'L MANAGER.

E. H. HINTON,
TRAFFIC MANAGER.

One of the longer bridges on the railroad was a five-span trestle over the Caney Fork River just west of the Buffalo Valley community. The original structure, dating from the late 1890s, was a swing-span type drawbridge that was opened when steamboat service was operating. The bridge was later heavily damaged by a torrential flood in 1902, washing out the swing span. A new, heavier span was built to replace it later that same year. The structure is pictured undergoing reconstruction. (Both, Monterey Depot Museum.)

This view, facing east, shows the Tennessee Central track about three miles east of Nashville around 1912 near Omohundro waterworks. The piles of wood and steel in the foreground are for the construction of the massive Lewisburg & Northern Railroad bridge, which would span both the TC and the Cumberland River. (Author's collection.)

Throughout its corporate history, the TC purchased most of its motive power from the American Locomotive Company of Schenectady, New York. One of the first to be purchased new by the railroad was No. 202, delivered in 1903. Note that the cab is lettered "T.C.R.R."—before the company's 1922 reorganization. (ALCO Historic Photos.)

A westbound TC freight train pulled by two locomotives glides through Cookeville in 1907. The city's original two-story frame depot, dating to the original Nashville & Knoxville Railroad era, can be seen at far right. Two years later, this was replaced by an attractive brick station that survives today. (Tennessee State Library & Archives.)

From left to right, the train crew of Charlie Hays, Bill Loftis, and Bill Manning pose in front of No. 6 near South Carthage around 1910. This was one of eight 4-4-0 types on the railroad's roster. This locomotive was one of the oldest, built in 1882 for the TC predecessor Nashville & Knoxville Railroad, but still more than adequate for switching cars in branch line service. (Dr. W.O. Greene III collection.)

Above, during the 1920s, while switching cars on the depot house track at Monterey, a train crew takes time to pose with a visiting mother and her two young sons. In the early 20th century, railroads were not as safety-conscious as in later years; employees were very accommodating when it came to letting visitors pose on locomotives and rolling stock. The crew includes the engineer (standing on the locomotive), two flagmen, a conductor, and a fireman. Below, TC No. 9, a 4-4-0 type built during the 1880s, is in Smith County with its crew. (Both, Monterey Depot collection.)

After bringing their train in from Carthage, the crew and other TC employees pose by an unidentified locomotive in front of the Carthage Junction depot around 1915. This station was where the 7.5-mile Carthage branch diverged from the Eastern Division's main track. The branch predated the TC, having been built by the N&K Railroad in the early 1890s. (Dr. John Payne collection.)

A railroad crew proudly poses with TC No. 14 at an unknown location with a visitor and his two young sons around 1918. The 2-8-0 was built by ALCO in 1902 and later renumbered. As cameras became smaller and more affordable for many Americans after 1910, people enjoyed having their photographs taken with the massive locomotives and train crews. (Dr. John Payne collection.)

Hickman was a small but vibrant farming town whose businesses and customers were all connected to agriculture in some way. The TC's facilities here consisted of the main track, passing track, a spur that could accommodate several freight cars, and a combination depot, which is out of view. (Dr. W.O. Greene III collection.)

This small wood caboose, one of several purchased by the TC during the 1900s, is an example of the investment by the railroad in new locomotives, rolling stock, and infrastructure during its early years. For over a century, these cars, normally located at the end of a freight train, served as an office for the train crew, including the conductor, brakeman, and flagman. (National Archives of Canada collection.)

This image is a bit of a mystery, but it appears to be a staged photograph taken in Putnam County around 1920. The blurred smoke indicates this was a longer exposure and No. 31 was not moving. TC records indicate the locomotive was built in 1899, one of several 2-8-0 types operating on the railroad at this time. (Tennessee State Library & Archives.)

Train No 5, the Shopping Train, visible at far left behind the trees, approaches TC's Nashville depot in 1915. The First National Bank and Stahlman Building can be seen in the city's skyline. The curvy track in the foreground was used by the railroad to transfer freight to riverboats. (Tennessee State Library & Archives.)

TC No. 205 and its crew are seen at an unknown location. The man at left appears to be a flagman, while the one at center wearing a three-piece suit is definitely a superintendent or other high-ranking railroad official. The engineer is at right. It was common for the company photographer to take pictures of employees with their train on special occasions, such as an employee's promotion or retirement. The locomotive pictured was built by ALCO and was one of several of this type acquired new by the TC in 1903. (Dr. John Payne collection.)

During the early 20th century, before workplace safety was mandated, the railroad industry was plagued by serious accidents and derailments; the primary objective of railroad managers was to keep the trains running and on schedule. During the pre-dawn hours of October 30, 1919, a TC freight originating in Monterey was traveling on the Crawford branch with a 20-car train. As it passed over a wooden trestle near the Lovejoy community, the center of the bridge suddenly collapsed, sending the last 13 cars into the ravine below. The two brakemen riding on top of the train were crushed underneath the wreckage and killed. The accident was partially blamed on the conductor of a passenger train from the previous day who did not report a derailment he had witnessed near the bridge. (Both, Monterey Depot Museum.)

Three

A GLORIOUS ERA

After a full year of operation, all of the TC was open for business with the dedication of the Western Division between Nashville and Hopkinsville in October 1903. A few months later, however, the railroad encountered many challenges that tested the company's ability to survive. On New Year's Eve 1903, a devastating fire erupted at TC's East Yard in Nashville, destroying the roundhouse and several other structures. The railroad did not have enough insurance to cover the extensive damage. Less than two months later, on February 29, 1904, the man dubbed the "father of the Tennessee Central," Jere Baxter, died suddenly. Months after Baxter's death, the TC was struggling with debt. Finally, in March of that year, the TC was in receivership. In 1905, the Standard Trust Company optioned to buy the TC but, to protect their rail connections, the Illinois Central Railroad and Southern Railway leased the Western and Eastern Divisions, respectively. This arrangement lasted for three years. The TC was reorganized and ultimately resumed independent operation of its line in 1908. Over the next several years, the TC continued to deal with debt. The railroad was placed in receivership, remaining in that status for eight more years. After suffering years of losses, the TC was sold to new owners in early 1922. The new name was changed to Tennessee Central Railway. Now with new management, the railroad wasted no time replacing its aging locomotives and rolling stock. Another cost-saving measure by the TC was the restructuring of passenger service. Management soon discontinued under-performing trains such as the popular Shopping Train between Nashville and Monterey and the overnight train between Nashville and Hopkinsville. In addition, dedicated branch line passenger service was replaced by mixed-train service, which consisted of a freight train carrying a passenger car. The TC received its first diesel engine on December 5, 1939. Built by ALCO, the unit was also the first diesel engine placed into service in Nashville.

A wreck train crew poses for a quick photograph at Emory Gap before going to work. The train consisted of TC's first steam-powered wrecker, No. W2076; specially-outfitted flatcar No. 2078; a tool car; and a caboose. Wreck trains were equipped to clear tracks of debris or damaged equipment from the track or right-of-way following a derailment. Notice the wheelsets on top of the second car. (Monterey Depot Museum.)

A brakeman returns to his train after realigning the switch at Monterey following a meeting with an opposing train during the 1930s. The yard at Monterey was always busy, going back to the days of TC's predecessor, the Nashville & Knoxville Railroad. The facility once had a roundhouse, sand tower, coal chute, and several maintenance buildings. (John W. Barriger III photograph, Barriger National Railroad Library, University of Missouri–St. Louis [UMSL].)

The TC frequently placed newspaper advertisements in cities it served. This full-page ad dates from 1929 and emphasizes industrial development and improvements the company had made to improve service. It was around this time that the railroad started using a new slogan, "The Road of Personal Service," perhaps to distinguish it from larger and less-folksy railroads. The biggest threat to TC's future business was not other railroads but competition from trucks. Paved roads and an improved highway system led to the rapid expansion of the trucking industry. Passenger service is barely mentioned in this ad; ridership on trains had been reduced dramatically in recent years. The Nashville-to-Harriman service was down to two daily roundtrips. The train between Nashville and Hopkinsville was discontinued the following year. (Author's collection.)

From the beginning, TC was built to haul coal as its primary commodity. As a result, the first cars purchased were hopper cars, similar to the one shown here, an external-braced wood car built by the American Car and Foundry of St. Louis. In later years, the design of hopper cars improved, and capacity increased after the cars were built of steel. (National Archives of Canada collection.)

For many years, a small portion of the freight hauled by the TC was livestock. The railroad operated several stock cars to transport livestock from customers until the late 1940s. Many of the cars rostered by the railroad, such as this external-braced version built in 1926, were built by the Pressed Steel Car Company of Pittsburgh, Pennsylvania. (National Archives of Canada collection.)

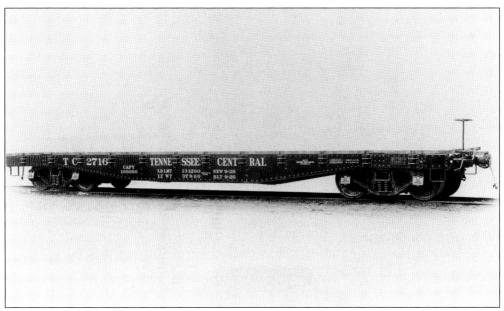

In 1926, several flatcars were purchased by the TC to haul freight that was too large or bulky to fit in a traditional 40-foot boxcar. This fleet of cars was built by the Pressed Steel Car Company. (National Archives of Canada collection.)

For over a hundred years, boxcars have been a common sight on freight trains. Originally constructed of wood, steel boxcars were preferred after 1920 because of the risk of fire and the limitation of the size and weight of freight that could be carried. This external braced car was rebuilt at the TC shops in Nashville in 1938. (National Archives of Canada collection.)

Locomotive No. 506 switches cars at the yard in Emory Gap during a hazy afternoon in the mid-1940s. The 506 was one of several locomotives purchased new by the railroad during its formative years. (Dr. John Payne collection.)

Shortly after the first TC train rolled into Nashville, the company ordered six class 4-6-0 locomotives from ALCO. These were put into service in 1903. One of these, No. 502, is pictured in Nashville in 1940. Nine years later, the handsome locomotive was retired with other coal burners, bumped by a fleet of new ALCO diesel FA-1 locomotives. (Dr. John Payne collection.)

Located on top of the Cumberland Plateau, Crossville is one of the larger cities served by the TC and one of the few to be graced with a brick station. At one time, the line served several customers in the area, each with its own spur track. The railroad can be seen cutting through the downtown area in 1940. The depot is conveniently located where the track bisects Main Street. The attractive Cumberland County Courthouse is visible at left. (Tennessee State Library & Archives.)

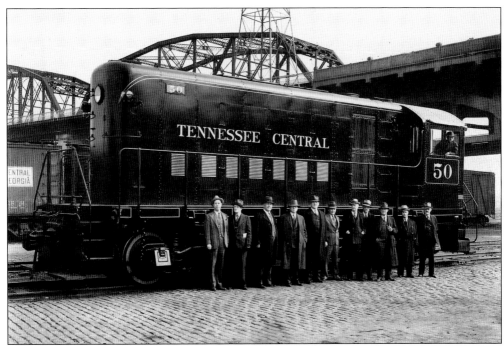

Railroad officials and Nashville city leaders pose in front of TC No. 50, the company's first diesel locomotive, on December 5, 1939. The locomotive was placed on display at First Avenue and Broadway near the passenger depot. The unit was the first diesel placed into service in middle Tennessee. (Tennessee State Library & Archives.)

During the early 1940s, TC acquired several former New York Central locomotives for use between Nashville and Harriman. No. 728 and another former New York Central engine are pictured being serviced at Monterey before their next assignment. These locomotives were some of the heaviest and most powerful on the railroad. (Monterey Depot Museum.)

During a rainy and overcast day, a photographer looking east from the rear of his train captured this view of Monterey's yard and facilities in the late 1930s. In the distance, an eastbound passenger train to Harriman is stopping to take on water. On the right, two locomotives wait for their next assignment. (John W. Barriger III photograph, Barriger National Railroad Library, UMSL.)

A group of seasoned railroad men take time to pose with their train on the Eastern Division. While the names of these crewmen have been lost to history, the way they are dressed and the expressions on their faces say a lot. Their work was very dangerous and physically difficult, but the men were proud of their positions with the TC. They were family. (Dr. W.O. Greene III collection.)

After receiving a fresh coat of paint at the Nashville shops, No. 729 poses for its portrait during the early 1940s. It was one of six former New York Central locomotives purchased by the TC. (Dr. John Payne collection.)

There are several stations with unusual names along the TC but none more unique than Sebowisha. Located between Carthage Junction and Lancaster, the station consisted of a shelter and cinder platform. Nearby, a stairway led up a cliff to a hilltop lodge, visible on the left. TC officials brought customers, railroad brass, or occasionally politicians here to be entertained—primarily with hunting, drinking, or other diversions. (John W. Barriger III photograph, Barriger National Railroad Library, UMSL.)

The TC purchased an additional diesel switcher, No. 51, from ALCO in 1941. Designated as a class S1, the locomotive was assigned to switch cars at industries and yards around Nashville. Its color scheme of maroon and gold matched that of No. 50, delivered to the railroad two years earlier. This builder's photograph shows the locomotive at the ALCO plant in Schenectady before being delivered to the TC. (ALCO Historic Photos.)

The transition from steam to diesel power on the TC occurred over a five-year period beginning with the delivery of three Baldwin units in 1948. During the next eight years, 19 new diesel locomotives were on the property. The last steam engine was retired in 1954. In the early 1950s, Nos. 506 and 333 bask in the sun at the Nashville roundhouse between assignments. (Dr. John Payne collection.)

This five-span bridge over the Caney Fork River has been repaired and modified several times since the 1890s. Its appearance has changed little since this picture was taken around 1920. The bridge remains in use for freight trains today. The photographer neglected to move his bags, visible at right, out of the picture. (Tennessee State Library & Archives.)

During a station stop at Emory Gap, the train's fireman chats with another employee before returning to his cab. Soon, No. 554 will take eastbound No. 2 the few remaining miles to Harriman, the end of the run. (Monterey Depot Museum.)

In the early 1940s, the shop crew at Nashville pose with No. 553, a 1926 product of ALCO. Steam locomotives were labor intensive, requiring several workers to keep the behemoths in running order. Following the trend of larger railroads, the TC transitioned to diesel power during the early 1950s to increase efficiency and also to cut labor costs. (James D. Le Croy collection.)

Of all the special trains TC operated over the years, troop trains were always a priority when the nation was at war. H.W. Stanley, president of the TC, and an unidentified employee discuss an upcoming troop movement over the railroad with an Army officer in the mid-1940s. (Tennessee State Library & Archives.)

FAST PASSENGER AND FREIGHT SCHEDULES

via

The Tennessee Central Railway

In the 1940s, railroads were still a preferred mode of transportation, for both shipping goods and traveling. In this advertisement, the TC mentions its direct connections with the Illinois Central Railroad at Hopkinsville on the west, and with the Southern Railway at Harriman on the east. However, the ad fails to mention that the road also connected with both the Louisville & Nashville and the Nashville, Chattanooga & St. Louis in Nashville. This omission was probably intentional; the L&N and NC&StL were fierce competitors for rail traffic in the region and did little to promote one another. (Author's collection.)

Mikado No. 703 is at Monterey during a layover in the late 1940s. The 2-8-2 was one of several former New York Central Railroad locomotives purchased by the TC during the late 1930s and early 1940s. The Imperial Hotel is partially visible at left. (Monterey Depot Museum.)

During much of the 20th century, specifically the 1920s through the 1950s, railroads were the primary mode of transportation for both passengers and freight. As part of their marketing efforts to attract new customers, companies often gave out promotional items such as calendars and pencils. The TC was a smaller company and had a limited budget for advertising. Since smoking was commonplace at the time, the company gave away ashtrays and matchbooks. These small trinkets were inexpensive but got the company's name and logo in front of customers. (Author's collection.)

This photograph was taken on a hazy, warm evening at dusk at a time when freight trains still stopped for water and passengers could board trains 1 and 2 here. The depot agent knew the first names of the train crews. It had been that way for a long time. However, over the next few years, things would change. By the mid-1950s, steam locomotives were replaced by diesels. The TC's lone passenger train, between Nashville and Harriman, was discontinued in mid-1955. The operator continued to hand up train orders to the crews as the engines roared by, but it was not the same. (Cumberland County Archives and Family Heritage Center collection.)

Four

DEPOTS, STRUCTURES, AND FACILITIES

While most railroad histories focus on locomotives, rolling stock, and all types of train equipment, the company's physical plant—stations, coaling towers, water tanks, and other miscellaneous trackside structures—are too often ignored. In spite of the modest size of its territory, at one time, the TC had approximately 100 stations along its main line and five branches. Nearly all of these depots were staffed by an agent and other personnel. However, by the late 1930s, as a cost-saving measure, the railroad replaced lower-volume depots with simple unstaffed passenger shelters. Twenty years later, after passenger service had ceased, only a handful of the depots along the TC remained staffed, such as Lebanon, Carthage Junction, Cookeville, Monterey, and others. This was essential not only to handle existing freight and express business at busier agencies, but also so operators could pass on important information to the crews of passing trains using train orders. In a time before centralized traffic control and two-way radios, train orders were the key means of communications on the TC, even through the 1960s. The train orders were held out to crews of passing trains using a "hoop." After the arrival of diesel locomotives in the early 1950s, numerous coaling towers, water tanks, turntables, and switchman's shanties, all once common sights along the right-of-way and necessary for steam locomotive operation, were now redundant and soon retired by the TC. The lower costs of diesel operations, both in facilities and labor, resulted in substantial savings for the railroad. Few of these picturesque buildings were photographed before being demolished. What follows are images of facilities and structures from across the railroad.

Nashville's small TC passenger depot was opened around 1902 and consisted of an L-shaped wood-frame building. It had two platforms that served three stub-end tracks. The station had a small waiting room, ticket booth, baggage room, and office for crew members and other TC employees. While waiting for their train, passengers could grab a quick snack at the restaurant, which served sandwiches, short orders, and beverages. When rail travel was at its busiest, around 1908, the terminal was served by eight daily departures and an equal number of arrivals—five trains on the Eastern Division and two on the Western. After 1930, traffic was down to two daily departures. Regular passenger service ended on July 31, 1955. These images were taken in 1963, weeks before the station was demolished. (Both, Bruce Meyer.)

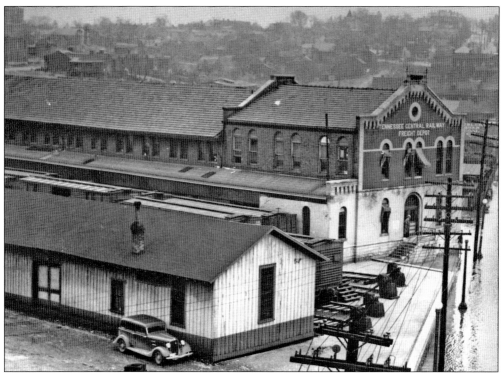

The 1902 freight depot in downtown Nashville was one of the most impressive structures on the TC's system. The two-story building was faced with brick and stone, topped with a Spanish-tiled roof, and was nearly a half block in length. During the early hours of December 5, 1942, a fire destroyed the entire structure and its contents, including freight stored in the building's warehouse. Another casualty of the blaze was the TC's complete corporate history and all records, dating back 45 years, stored in the offices. The picture below shows the modern replacement structure that opened in 1943. The new freight house was built on the same site as the previous one but featured a flat roof and a single-story warehouse. (Both, Tennessee State Library & Archives.)

The first station east of Nashville's downtown depot was "Shops," located two miles away at TC's main yard. The Shops building served as both a yard office and depot and was on the north side of the main track. In 1956, the Shops building was retired and replaced by a modern building on the opposite side of the track. (John W. Barriger III photograph, Barriger National Railroad Library, UMSL.)

The railroad's shops and main maintenance facility were east of downtown Nashville on Fairfield Avenue, later renamed Willow Street. In the years after this 1930s scene was recorded, several improvements were made to the TC's yard that included a new master mechanics building and an open car repair shed. Nashville's City Hospital is visible in the background. (Tennessee State Library & Archives .)

In the early days of passenger service, the TC had fully-staffed depots at most of the communities it served. As the railroad struggled with finances during the 1930s, it sought ways to cut costs. By the early 1940s, the company had replaced many of its less-patronized depots with simple shelters, such as this one at Donelson. (Bob Bell Jr.)

The TC's depot at Mt. Juliet was similar in architectural style to the standard wood-frame structures in Lebanon, Rockwood, and others across the railroad. For over 30 years, this community was served by both the TC and the Nashville, Chattanooga & St. Louis Railway, which served different stations that were almost adjacent to one another. (Wilson County Archives.)

The TC's combination depot in Lebanon was always busy with passenger and freight business as well as being a Railway Express Agency office. In the background, several boxcars are on the station's house track, while at far right, an REA truck has backed up to the dock preparing to unload boxes. (Wilson County Archives.)

While not officially a TC depot, the original Nashville, Chattanooga & St. Louis Railway station at Lebanon was jointly served by the TC-predecessor Nashville & Knoxville Railroad and the NC&StL. Passengers could transfer trains here to continue their journey between Nashville and Harriman. The station was destroyed by fire in 1971. (Tennessee State Library & Archives.)

The handsome combination depot at Watertown was one of only a few on the TC system to be constructed of brick, replacing a wood station destroyed by fire the previous year. The photograph above was taken shortly after the building opened in 1924. The structure was unusually large to be serving such a small community. Two years later, the railroad opened a depot in Crossville with a similar design. Below, the freight and express portion of the building is shown from the opposite side decades later. In addition to the impressive station, the railroad also had a water tank and a turntable in the 1920s. The station was demolished in 1972. (Above, Wilson County Archives; below, Bob Bell Jr.)

The North Alexandria depot was actually located in the Brush Creek community; the TC reportedly renamed it before 1923 to attract more business from the larger town of Alexandria a few miles south. The combination station had a siding and a house track for storing cars. When this photograph was taken in the early 1960s, the agency had already been closed and the building abandoned. (Dr. W.O. Greene III collection.)

The Carthage Junction depot is situated where TC's Carthage branch, at left, diverges from the Nashville to Harriman main line near Gordonsville. The "witch's hat" roof design was unique, not found on any other depots on the railroad. In recent years, the unusual depot has been relocated near Carthage and now houses a train museum. (Author photograph.)

A local TC freight prepares to leave the freight office at South Carthage in the early 1960s The TC's Carthage branch never physically served its namesake city but ended on the opposite side of the Cumberland River at South Carthage. The simple office building pictured replaced a larger combination station demolished around 1940 for the widening of US Route 70 North. (Bob Bell Jr.)

Silver Point once boasted both a passenger depot and freight house. For many years, the community had a lucrative livestock business; there were also several trackside stock pens during the 1930s. The station was a staging point for helper locomotives that assisted heavy freights to negotiate the steep grades of Silver Point hill. (John W. Barriger III photograph, Barriger National Railroad Library, UMSL.)

The combination depot at Baxter was a primary station for TC passenger trains as well as a busy freight agency that had a house track for loading and unloading freight cars. This remained an open agency until the late 1960s. The building was demolished in 1969. (Monterey Depot Museum.)

The Cookeville passenger station opened in 1909 to great fanfare, replacing a two-story wood structure built by the predecessor Nashville & Knoxville Railroad. Architecturally, the brick passenger station was unique, sporting a roof with an Asian-type influence. This station has been restored and now houses a local museum. West of the station, the TC also once had a track scale and a wye for turning locomotives. Industrial spurs served many industries in the area. The image below shows the water tank and freight depot just west of the passenger station. (Above, Tennessee State Library & Archives; below, John W. Barriger III photograph, Barriger National Railroad Library, UMSL.)

The Algood depot was one of the oldest on the TC, dating from the 19th century when it was built by the Nashville & Knoxville Railroad. The station also served trains of the Overton County Railroad, later renamed the Tennessee, Kentucky & Northern Railroad, until the late 1920s. (Cookeville History Museum collection.)

Monterey was an important station for the TC, located just west of the junction where the Crawford branch diverged. A heavy volume of coal hoppers from nearby mines on the branch came through here over the years, generating substantial revenue for the road. This depot opened around 1903, replacing an earlier structure. (Monterey Depot collection.)

During the steam era, there were several coaling towers along TC's system. The most modern and unusual of these was at Monterey. The station was a major maintenance and servicing center for the railroad. This impressive structure remained well into the era of dieselization. (Author's collection.)

Throughout the steam locomotive era, it was common to see numerous water tanks along the railroad. After the TC converted to diesel locomotives, it was no longer necessary for trains to stop for water. By the late 1950s, most of these relics had been removed, with only a few remaining, such as this one at Crab Orchard. (Dr. W.O. Greene III collection.)

The depot at Crab Orchard was a busy agency, primarily because of the nearby limestone quarry that generated much business for the railroad for decades. During the era of TC's passenger service, all trains made a stop here. The depot was built on an embankment and was supported on posts. (Bob Bell Jr.)

The brick depot at Crossville was arguably one of the TC's more handsome stations, having been completed in 1926. Although the track though Crossville was removed in 1989 during the line's abandonment between here and Crab Orchard by the Norfolk Southern, the building was repurposed for non-railroad business and survives today. (Cumberland County Archives and Family Heritage Center collection.)

The combination station at Rockwood was believed to be the newest on the TC. The board-and-batten structure opened in 1937 to replace one destroyed by fire several years earlier. The agency was a busy one, serving the many nearby industries including the sprawling Roane Iron Company. It was razed in the mid-1960s. (Dr. W.O. Greene III collection.)

In spite of the mountainous terrain and numerous trestles, the TC had only one tunnel on its system, approximately four miles west of Rockwood. This bore allowed the railroad to go under Mount Roosevelt, avoiding extremely steep grades. Over the years, it has required strengthening and rebuilding to keep it operational. A unique feature of the tunnel is the decorative stone "TC" letters above each portal. (Monterey Depot collection.)

The curved mixed-span bridge near Rockwood is one of several impressive structures on the TC's east end. It takes the main line over several narrow-gauge ore tracks leading to the Roane Iron Company. This view dates from the early 1900s. (Louisville and Nashville Railroad Company Records, University Archives and Records Center, University of Louisville.)

A variety of smaller structures could be found trackside along the TC system. These buildings varied in size and purpose. The abandoned building above, seen at an unidentified location, may have served as a shanty for a flagman or switchman. Below, a similar but larger structure was probably used by the maintenance-of-way department providing storage for tools and equipment. (Both, Dr. W.O. Greene III collection.)

Just northwest of downtown Nashville, the TC had a smaller yard at Herman Street and Eleventh Avenue North that included a yard office and several other buildings. Here, trains are staged for switching customers such as the Kerrigan Iron Works, seen at right. Located on the two-mile Hamilton Street spur connecting the "belt line" to the Union Stock Yards, crews stayed busy serving numerous industries along the line. (Dr. John Payne collection.)

By the 1950s, the financial woes of the TC were seen in the form of deferred maintenance of buildings and tracks across its system. The abandoned Jefferson Street yard office on Nashville's northwest side was awaiting eventual demolition when this photograph was taken. (G. Battle Claiborne.)

For decades, the agency at Ashland City served many customers in the community. Since the 1920s, railroad crossties were processed, stored, and loaded onto flatcars on the station's house track, visible at right. In the image below, taken around the same time, stacks of crossties and their proximity to the depot and water tank are more evident. (Above, John W. Barriger III photograph, Barriger National Railroad Library, UMSL; below, Dr. John Payne collection.)

The TC's route through downtown Clarksville utilized several bridges and cuts to access its block-long combination station, shown at the center of this 1941 view. While the railroad's last passenger train to Clarksville was discontinued in 1930, the agency remained very busy and continued to have a lot of freight business as well as military trains destined for nearby Camp Campbell. The city was also served by the Louisville & Nashville Railroad's line between Bowling Green, Kentucky, and Memphis. Each railroad had its own depot and yard. Clarksville was the second largest city served by the TC behind Nashville. (Tennessee State Library & Archives.)

This 1930s view looks north, or railroad west, toward the approach of the TC's bridge across the Louisville & Nashville Railroad tracks and yard at Clarksville. This was one of several bridges the railroad used to negotiate the city's hilly terrain. The TC's depot is one mile ahead. (John W. Barriger III photograph, Barriger National Railroad Library, UMSL.)

The TC's Clarksville depot, at left, was unusual in several aspects—it was the railroad's only two-story combination station and also the only structure on the Western Division to be made of brick. This 1930s scene faces north and shows the wood pedestrian bridge that provided access between the depot and the downtown area, visible on the far right. (John W. Barriger III photograph, Barriger National Railroad Library, UMSL.)

Repurposing a rail car for office space was a common practice for railroads. To cut costs at the East Yard Edgoten, Kentucky, station, a boxcar body was pressed into service by the TC, replacing an older combination depot. This also facilitated the opening of the agency to serve Camp Campbell, then under construction, as the nation's involvement in World War II grew more imminent. Edgoten soon became a busy interchange for the military installation after a new spur diverged from the main track to serve the numerous warehouses at the post. The unique metal shed above the roof provided additional protection from the hot sun, keeping the agent inside a bit cooler. The facility was intended to be temporary until a new office could be built but remained in operation into the mid-1960s. (Both, Dr. W.O. Greene collection.)

Five

TC's Nashville Terminal

The Nashville Terminal Company was incorporated and later leased to the TC in 1902 to build the depot and yards in Nashville. This company was often confused with another by the same name, owned by the Louisville & Nashville Railroad. Over time, TC's main line and spurs around the city were referred to as TC's Nashville Terminal. The TC's routing through Nashville was a rambling, circuitous one that requires explaining. It was always Jere Baxter's intention to build a direct route through Nashville connecting the Eastern and Western Divisions from Harriman to Hopkinsville. Baxter had intended for the main track to follow the west bank of the Cumberland River along Front Street, passing near the east side of the city's Public Square. From there the TC would continue north, crossing the Louisville & Nashville Railroad before turning west and paralleling Harrison Street. From this point, the railroad would head northwest toward Clarksville and points north. Baxter did not anticipate the fierce opposition he would face from the Louisville & Nashville Railroad, which held a virtual monopoly in the region. This may or may not have factored into Nashville's decision to pass an ordinance prohibiting the TC from using its Front Street track as part of its extension north. As a result, the railroad was forced to build a substantially longer line around the entire city to connect the two lines. Over the years, this route around Nashville was referred to as "the belt line" by employees. The belt line diverged from the Eastern Division approximately two miles east of downtown at a point called Belt Line Junction. On the opposite side of town, it connected with the Western Division at East Side Junction. These interchanges were renamed in 1905 as Southern Junction and Central Junction, respectively. In addition to the belt line, the TC also had a West Nashville spur, just over two miles in length, and the Hamilton Street spur, two miles long. The Nashville area had nearly 18 miles of track.

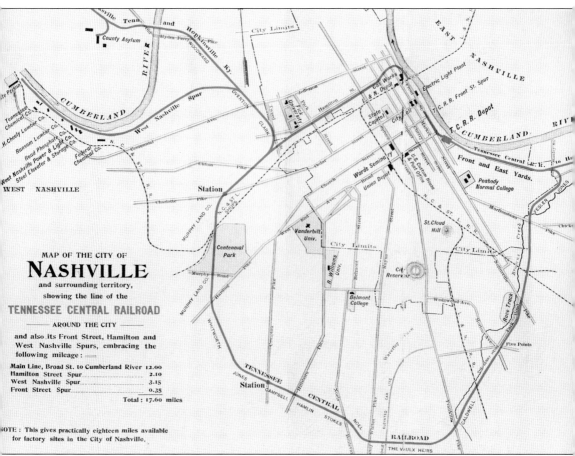

Although the TC never had quite the presence in Nashville as the Louisville & Nashville Railroad and its affiliated Nashville, Chattanooga & St. Louis Railway, Jere Baxter's line surrounded the city on three sides with its meandering belt line, which provided a connection between the road's Eastern and Western Divisions between Southern Junction and Central Junction, respectively. Built between 1902 and 1903, the belt line, along with its multiple spurs and sidings, comprised approximately 18 miles of trackage in and around Nashville. During the road's early days, TC employees referred to this as the Nashville Terminal, often confused with L&N's Nashville Terminal Railroad. This 1902 map shows the circuitous routing of the TC around Nashville due to the powerful influence of the Louisville & Nashville Railroad. The L&N ultimately stopped Jere Baxter from building his railroad through the city. Ever determined, Baxter succeeded in pushing north to Hopkinsville. (Historic Rugby Inc. collection.)

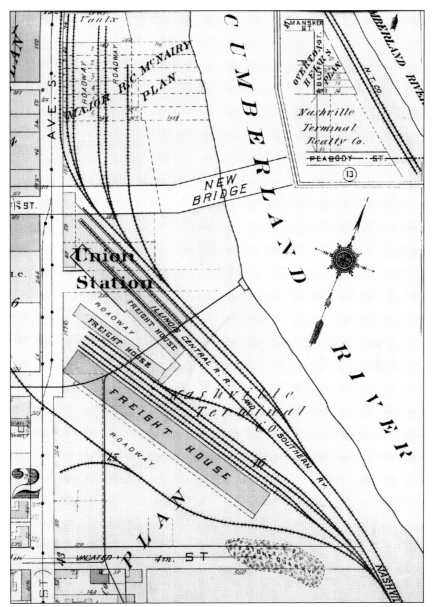

When the Standard Trust Company optioned to buy the TC in 1905, the Illinois Central Railroad leased the Western Division of the railroad while the Southern Railway leased the Eastern Division. This arrangement lasted until 1908, when the company was reorganized as the Tennessee Central Railroad. The Nashville station was briefly referred to as "Union Station," creating much confusion with the city's main Union Station. This 1908 map provides a good understanding of the TC's property in the heart of Nashville between 1902 and 1922. Other than railroad ownership, the area remained relatively unchanged during this period. The simple wood passenger station at center fronted First Avenue along with the adjacent freight houses. Between these buildings and the river was TC's Front Street Yard, which consisted of several spur tracks. In 1908, this changed dramatically with the construction of the Shelby Street Bridge. In 1921, the rail yard was altered to accommodate the new river and rail terminal at the foot of Broadway, a facility that expedited freight movement between trains and barges. (Metro Nashville Archives.)

The opening of the Bryan River and Rail Terminal in 1922 began a new era of water and rail transportation. The $300,000 facility, designed by the Foster & Creighton Company, was named after Judge M.T. Bryan, a widely known river enthusiast, and was located at Broadway and First Avenue South. The five-story terminal served as a transloading center and warehouse where freight could be interchanged between river barges and railcars of the TC. Construction is well underway in late 1921 in the image above. Below, in a scene from the 1940s, boxcars and barges are seen on the riverside. The crane was used to transfer cargo between the two. (Both, Creighton collection, Metro Nashville Archives.)

The late 1930s view above looks north down First Avenue along Nashville's riverfront toward Broadway. The track on the left side of the street belongs to the Nashville Railway and Light Company, the operator of the Nashville streetcar line. The track to the right of it is the TC's Front Street spur, which served the warehouses between Broadway and Union Street. On the right, railcars are staged at TC's Front Street Yard adjacent to Bryan River and Rail Terminal. Below, a photograph taken from the same vantage point affords a better view of the TC's Front Street Yard and the river. The Cumberland River Sand Company can be seen in the distance where the barge is docked. (Both, John W. Barriger III photograph, Barriger National Railroad Library, UMSL.)

This aerial view from the mid-1950s illustrates the major presence the TC had in downtown Nashville and on the west bank of the Cumberland River for more than 60 years. Bryan River and Rail Terminal is at upper left near the intersection of First Avenue and Broadway. At center is the railroad's Front Street Yard. Shelby Street Bridge, which goes over the tracks, connected

downtown with East Nashville and was completed in 1908. To the right of the bridge are the passenger depot and freight house. Today, this bridge is a popular pedestrian crossing that connects to the city's extensive greenway and trail system. (Metro Nashville Archives.)

The TC's Nashville freight house was the newest building constructed by the railroad, having replaced a previous one destroyed by fire in 1942. The two-story terminal measured 50 feet in width and 500 feet in length. The front of the terminal contained railroad offices with a warehouse section at the rear. In this image, boxcars are spotted at the side dock. (G. Battle Claiborne.)

In late December 1926, Nashville experienced a historic flood, which took a toll on parts of the city closest to the Cumberland River. This view shows TC's passenger depot and freight house underwater during the disaster. Fortunately, the railroad had enough advance notice to remove all freight from the buildings and move its trains to higher ground. (Metro Nashville Archives.)

This 1950s aerial view shows Southern Junction, where TC's Western Division diverges from the Eastern Division near Nashville's city limits. This was the east end of TC's belt line, which takes the railroad around the entire city before heading northwest toward Hopkinsville. Note the various buildings and abandoned passenger cars inside the interchange. Hermitage Avenue can be seen at bottom. (Author's collection.)

The meandering TC belt line through Nashville was a constant source of aggravation for the city's motorists, especially during rush hour. The track crossed five major highways at grade. Because of all the curves along the 11-mile loop, trains typically moved very slowly, regularly creating traffic bottlenecks. In this scene, cars on Lafayette Street are stopped by a Hopkinsville–bound freight train in 1951. (Metro Nashville Archives.)

The TC's primary yard and maintenance center was Nashville's East Yard, referred to as "Shops" in all railroad correspondence and timetables. Located near Hermitage and Fairfield Avenues, the sprawling facility contained a roundhouse, open car shed, master mechanic's office, blacksmith

shop, carpentry shop, and other outbuildings. Willow Street is above, and the yard office is at lower left. (Author's collection.)

This late 1920s scene shows the TC's belt line skirting the Nashville, Chattanooga & St. Louis Railway's sprawling "New Shops" in West Nashville. The NC&StL roundhouse is at upper right. In the lower left, the TC's Van Blarcom depot is visible where the curved track crosses Charlotte Avenue. For many years, incoming passengers from Clarksville and other points on the Western Division had the option of disembarking at Van Blarcom station and transferring to a Charlotte Avenue streetcar for a shorter and more direct ride downtown, saving at least 15 minutes versus the lengthier ride around the belt line to the TC's downtown depot. The station is named for J.C. Van Blarcom of St. Louis, an early investor in the railroad. At one time, the station was served by four daily passenger trains operating between Nashville and Hopkinsville. By 1930, all passenger service had been discontinued west of Nashville. A few years later, the depot was retired. (Metro-Nashville Archives.)

Six

PASSENGER SERVICE ON THE TC

The origins of passenger train service on the TC go back to the Nashville & Knoxville Railroad during the 1890s when service was established between Monterey and Lebanon. When the TC absorbed the N&K in 1902, the fledgling new road had passenger service on its entire system, including all of its branches. On the Eastern Division, a traveler had several trains to choose from. Train Nos. 1 and 2, the Day Express, provided day service between Nashville and Harriman; train Nos. 3 and 4, the Volunteer State Express, accommodated overnight passengers. On most main line services, trains consisted of a railway post office car, baggage-express car, and two coaches. The night train had similar accommodations but with the addition of a Pullman sleeper car that connected with the Southern Railway for through service to Knoxville. In addition to these runs, Nos. 7 and 8, the Shopping Train, was a local accommodation train operating between Nashville and Monterey. On the Western Division, two round trips, nameless trains, held down the schedules between Nashville and Hopkinsville. Eventually, all passenger train names were abolished for simplicity. By the late 1920s, the Great Depression took its toll on the road's passenger service. The "Shopper" was cut first, and all service on the Carthage and Crawford branches was reduced to mixed train service. On November 18, 1930, Nos. 11 and 14 were discontinued between Nashville and Hopkinsville, relegating the Western Division to freight-only status. The two Nashville Harriman runs plugged on for another 19 years. As highways improved, ridership on the two remaining trains decreased dramatically. As a result, the night train was discontinued on January 31, 1949. The future of TC's lone passenger train became doubtful when the US Postal Service announced that it would use trucks to transport mail instead of the RPO car on Nos. 1 and 2, effective November 1954. With the loss of its RPO car, a major source of revenue, the day train hung on for a few more months. The trains made their final runs on July 31, 1955, and the TC was now officially freight-only.

SLEEPING CAR SERVICE

——THE——
Tennessee Central Railroad
COMPANY

Will on Sunday, December 25th (Christmas Day) 1904, in connection with The Southern Railway Company, establish a

Daily Sleeping Car Service
——BETWEEN——
Nashville and Knoxville

On the following schedule:

East Bound—Leaves Nashville.................11:15 P. M.
　　　　　Arrives Knoxville.................8:15 A. M.
West Bound—Leaves Knoxville.................9:30 P. M.
　　　　　Arrives Nashville.................7:00 A. M.

Sleeper open at Front-street Station at 9 P. M.
Tickets on sale 204 North Cherry Street, opposite Maxwell House, or at Front-street Station.

E. H. HINTON,
Traffic Manager.

On December 25, 1904, the TC established through Pullman sleeping car service between Nashville and Knoxville. The sleepers connected with trains from the Southern Railway at Harriman for the eastern portion to Knoxville. This arrangement lasted nearly 45 years before the overnight trains were discontinued in 1949. Passengers could occupy the car more than an hour before the scheduled departure time in both cities. The sleeper car was managed by the Pullman Company and had a dedicated attendant to assist customers. Advertisements like this appeared in the Nashville and Knoxville papers to promote the new premium service. (Author's collection.)

An excursion train from Nashville to Monterey is stopped near Lancaster so passengers and crew can pose for a photograph around 1905. While the TC had passenger service over all of its lines at this time, part of the company's revenue came from operating special charter trips similar to this outing. (Louisville & Nashville Railroad Company Records, University Archives and Records Center, University of Louisville.)

Standing in the aisle, conductor Pete Mulvihill (left) and an unidentified flagman are seen taking tickets on a TC passenger train during the 1930s. This scene illustrates how uncomfortable train travel once was. The coaches were often crowded, the seats did not recline, and the ceiling lamps were dim. The only relief passengers had from the oppressive heat was the breeze from the open coach windows. (Tennessee State Library & Archives.)

An unidentified eastbound TC passenger train makes a station stop at Daysville around 1910. Several men are shown unloading a large crate from the combination railway post office car while curious passengers watch from the next car. This was a typical scene in early-20th-century rural America. (Monterey Depot Museum.)

A westbound passenger train accelerates away from Monterey's depot around 1917 as passengers gather. The depot was a center of activity for the community during the railroad's early days. Monterey is where the Crawford branch diverged from the Nashville–Harriman main line and was an important servicing location for steam locomotives. (Monterey Depot Museum.)

10	8	6	4	2	Mls	November 28, 1909.	1	3	7	5	9
PM	AM	PM	PM	AM	....	LEAVE] [ARRIVE	PM	AM	AM	AM	PM
†8 10	†10 45	*4 00	*8 30	*8 30	0	+..... **Nashville**[1] .... ð	8 45	6 15	7 50	10 00	2 10
8 15	10 50	4 05	8 35	8 35	2	....Southern Junction.. ð	8 40	6 10	7 45	9 55	2 05
8 24	10 59	4 14	– –	8 44	7	.........Harding.........	8 30	– –	7 37	9 46	1 55
8 28	11 01	4 17	– –	8 48	8	.... Donelson........	8 28	5 58	7 35	9 43	1 52
8 33	11 08	4 23	– –	8 53	11	.......Hermitage......	8 22	– –	7 29	9 38	1 45
8 37	11 13	4 28	– –	8 58	13	.......Tulip Grove.......	8 17	– –	7 25	9 33	1 40
8 42	11 18	4 33	– –	9 02	15	.....Green Hill.......	8 12	– –	7 20	9 28	1 35
8 46	11 22	4 38	10 00	9 06	17	...... Mount Juliet .... ð	8 07	5 38	7 15	9 23	1 30
8 55	11 30	4 48	– –	9 15	21	.... Beckwith	5 59	– –	7 07	9 15	1 23
7 00	11 36	4 52	10 19	9 20	23	.... Martha	5 55	5 25	7 00	9 10	1 17
7 08	11 43	4 59	10 26	9 30	27	... Horn Springs	5 48	5 18	6 51	9 01	1 10
7 20	11 55	5 10	10 57	9 43	32	+...... **Lebanon**[2] ...... ð	5 36	5 07	†6 40	8 47	†1 00
PM	AM	5 25	– –	9 56	37	...... Greenwood	5 25	– –	AM	8 34	PM
.....	.....	5 30	– –	10 01	39	...... Shop Springs	5 21	– –	.....	8 29	.....
.....	.....	5 41	– –	10 11	43	....Cherry Valley......	5 12	– –	.....	8 19	.....
.....	.....	5 48	11 04	10 15	45	+..... Watertown ...... ð	5 08	4 40	.....	8 15	.....
.....	.....	5 58	– –	10 26	49	...... Holmes Gap	4 57	– –	.....	8 05	.....
.....	.....	6 08	11 20	10 34	53	...... Brush Creek......	4 49	– –	.....	7 58	.....
.....	.....	6 13	– –	10 42	56	.... Sykes..........	4 42	– –	.....	7 50	.....
.....	.....	§6 40	11 37	10 49	59	.... Hickman	4 35	– –	.....	7 45	.....
.....	.....	6 48	11 42	10 55	61	.**Carthage Junction**[3] ð	4 29	4 05	.....	7 40	.....
.....	.....	6 58	11 58	11 06	66	+....Lancaster........	4 17	3 55	.....	7 28	.....
.....	.....	7 07	– –	11 14	69	......Caney Fork......	4 09	– –	.....	7 20	.....
.....	.....	7 12	12 08	11 18	70	......Buffalo Valley.... ð	4 07	3 38	.....	7 17	.....
.....	.....	7 24	– –	11 30	75	...... Silver Point..... ð	3 54	3 27	.....	7 06	.....
.....	.....	7 34	– –	11 40	79	.... Boma	3 43	3 17	.....	6 57	.....
.....	.....	7 41	12 47	11 47	82	.... Baxter ...... ð	3 36	3 10	.....	6 50	.....
.....	.....	7 47	12 55	11 53	85	..... Double Springs	3 29	3 04	.....	6 44	.....
.....	.....	7 59	1 07	12 05	90	+..... Cookeville....... ð	3 18	2 50	.....	6 30	.....
.....	.....	8 08	1 16	12 15	95	.... **Algood**[4]....... ð	3 08	2 42	.....	6 22	.....
.....	.....	8 18	– –	12 25	98	........Parragon........	2 57	– –	.....	6 15	.....
.....	.....	8 22	– –	12 30	100	...... Brotherton	2 52	2 30	.....	6 10	.....
.....	.....	8 34	– –	12 40	104	.... Bilbrey	2 41	2 20	.....	6 00	.....
.....	.....	8 45	1 50	†1 12	108	+..... **Monterey**[5] .... ð	2 30	2 10	.....	*5 50	.....
.....	.....	PM	2 00	1 23	113	.... Dripping Springs	2 20	2 00	.....	AM	.....
.....	.....	.....	2 05	1 29	115	.... Welch	2 15	1 54	.....	.....	.....
.....	.....	.....	2 10	1 35	117	...... Johnson Stand ... ð	2 11	1 51	.....	.....	.....
.....	.....	.....	2 12	1 38	119	..**Campbell Junction**[6].	2 08	1 47	.....	.....	.....
.....	.....	.....	2 20	1 45	122	......Pomona Road.......	2 02	1 37	.....	.....	.....
.....	.....	.....	2 30	1 55	126	.... Creston........	1 55	1 27	.....	.....	.....
.....	.....	.....	2 41	2 10	131	+......Crossville....... ð	1 45	1 15	.....	.....	.....
.....	.....	.....	2 51	2 22	135	.... Dorton	1 37	1 04	.....	.....	.....
.....	.....	.....	2 56	2 27	137	......Otter Creek......	1 31	12 57	.....	.....	.....
.....	.....	.....	3 00	2 39	142	......Crab Orchard.... ð	1 21	12 45	.....	.....	.....
.....	.....	.....	3 16	2 50	146	.... Ozone......... ð	1 11	12 34	.....	.....	.....
.....	.....	.....	– –	– –	148	..**Millstone Junction**[7].	– –	– –	.....	.....	.....
.....	.....	.....	3 21	2 57	149	.......Waldensia ..... ð	1 05	12 27	.....	.....	.....
.....	.....	.....	3 29	3 04	152	.... Westel	12 57	12 17	.....	.....	.....
.....	.....	.....	3 41	3 14	157	+......Rockwood ..... ð	12 46	12 03	.....	.....	.....
.....	.....	.....	3 47	3 22	160	...... Cardiff	12 38	11 52	.....	.....	.....
.....	.....	.....	3 54	3 35	163	..... **Emory Gap**[8] ... ð	12 30	11 41	.....	.....	.....
.....	.....	.....	4 00	3 45	166	arr.. +|**Harriman**[9] ð.lve.	*12 25	*11 30	.....	.....	.....
.....	.....	.....	AM	PM	....	(*Via Southern Ry.*)	Noon	PM	.....	.....	.....
.....	.....	.....	6 45	5 55	216	...... **Knoxville**	*10 05	*8 05	.....	.....	.....

During the early years of TC's operation, the road could boast of seven passenger trains in and out of Nashville each day, five operating over the Eastern Division. For the first few years, the trains on the longer runs were named. Train Nos. 1 and 2, the day trains between Nashville and Harriman, were the Day Express; their overnight counterparts, Nos. 3 and 4, were the Volunteer State Limited. By the early 1920s, the two short round trips between Nashville and Lebanon had been annulled. In 1922, Nos. 5 and 6, the popular Shopping Train, were discontinued between Nashville and Monterey. The overnight train continued to operate a through Pullman sleeper to Knoxville until the train was dropped in 1949. During the next five years, ridership fell dramatically on Nos. 1 and 2, the day train. To the credit of TC management, this remaining train continued to make numerous flag stops along the route until its discontinuance on July 31, 1955. (Author's collection.)

In 1916, a crowd waits as eastbound train No. 2 arrives in Watertown on a winter morning. On this somber occasion, newly enlisted soldiers will board the train to head for their deployment center during World War I. After the train's arrival, the throng of people, comprising much of the town's population, will see the young men off. The TC's passenger trains were very busy during times when the nation was at war. Many charter trains were used to transport troops to Camp Campbell or other military installations. During peacetime, National Guard units also used the TC to move reservists to their summer camp locations until the 1950s. (Both, Wilson County Archives.)

In the early 1920s, TC operated twice-daily passenger service between Nashville and Red Boiling Springs, consisting of train service from Nashville to Carthage, where passengers would transfer to dedicated cars for the remainder of the trip to the springs. This unique arrangement lasted only a brief time during the early 1920s before being discontinued. Advertisements like this appeared frequently in Nashville papers at the time. (Author's collection.)

$6.85 **RED BOILLING SPRINGS**
AND RETURN

TENNESSEE CENTRAL RAILROAD

Double Daily Train Service . . . . . Auto From Carthage

GOING TRIP

Leave Nashville . . . . 9:00 A. M.   4:20 P. M.
Arrive Red Boiling Springs . 2:10 P. M.   9:30 P. M.

RETURN TRIP

Leave Red Boiling Springs 5:30 A. M.   2:00 P. M.
Arrive Nashville . . . . 10:55 A. M.   7:45 P. M.

J. E. SHIPLEY, General Passenger Agent

In October 1923, TC officials announced plans for a new Nashville passenger depot. The improved terminal would have been at the foot of Broadway on the west bank of the Cumberland River. The first floor was to serve as the passenger station, and the upper floors would house general offices for the railroad. Alas, the attractive building never became a reality because of a lack of funding. (Charles B. Castner collection.)

During the height of the passenger train era, it was common for railroads to take publicity photos of their newest equipment. This composition, made especially for the TC, shows a pristine ALCO No. 554 and a five-car train posing for its portrait in 1926 at an unknown location. (Dr. W.O. Greene III collection.)

In addition to its regularly scheduled passenger trains, the TC operated many special excursions throughout the year. One such train is seen near Lancaster in 1941 consisting of several coaches, a caboose, and business car No. 100 bringing up the rear. The TC officers on the rear platform take in the summer air as one of the men enjoys a sandwich. (Dr. John Payne collection.)

Cookeville was one of the busier stations for TC passenger trains, having higher ridership due to the many students traveling to and from Tennessee Polytechnic Institute (today's Tennessee Technological University). Since the university and the city were about halfway between Nashville and Knoxville, students traveling from across Tennessee would use the train for dependable transportation, especially during bad weather. In this 1930s view, trackside bystanders watch a TC inspection train as it leaves Cookeville on a wintry day. The photographer, standing on the rear platform of the train's business car, has nicely captured the flavor of the railroad scape—the passenger station is at left, and visible in the background are a water tank and freight house. At the time this scene was recorded, the city was still served by four trains each day. (John W. Barriger III photograph, Barriger National Railroad Library, UMSL.)

A three-car charter train prepares to leave the Nashville depot for a tour of the Eastern Division to Harriman during the late 1930s. Often, these special trains served as inspection trips for railroad officers, prospective shippers, or perhaps politicians. The image above provides a good view of the train's baggage car as well as other coaches stored in the yard. On the right, several outside braced boxcars are lined up at the freight house. Nashville's City Hospital is visible on top of Rolling Mill Hill in the background. The image below shows a different perspective, including the express and passenger cars parked on adjacent tracks, and the deteriorating tar paper roof of the station and umbrella sheds. The photographer stood on the Shelby Street bridge to record these views. (Both, John W. Barriger III photograph, Barriger National Railroad Library, UMSL.)

On a summer morning, TC's No. 2 picks up speed as it leaves Nashville with a three-car train consisting of a railway post office car and two coaches. By afternoon, the train will reach its destination at Harriman, some 166 miles to the east. Just a few years later, diesels would replace the venerable steam engines. (Dr. John Payne collection.)

Train activity is heavy at TC's Nashville depot on this cold winter morning in 1944. The overnight train from Harriman (far left) had just arrived a few hours earlier. The second train from the right, No. 2, prepares to depart for its day run to Harriman as a passing locomotive pulls a string of freight cars from the Bryan River and Rail Terminal. (Dr. John Payne collection.)

Tennessee Central Railway

Passenger Train Service

In Effect Nov. 1, 1939

"The Road of Personal Service"

After the 1920s, Tennessee Central Railway passenger timetables were very plain and sometimes printed on color paper. By this time, the TC was operating only two round trips between Nashville and Harriman. The overnight trains, Nos. 3 and 4, offered through Pullman sleeper service to Knoxville utilizing Southern Railway connecting trains at Harriman for the remainder of the trip. This train was taken off in 1949. The remaining train, Nos. 1 and 2, held down the daytime trips for another six years before being discontinued on July 31, 1955. During the following years, the TC had much success operating charter and excursion trains, something the railroad continued to do until 1967. (Author's collection.)

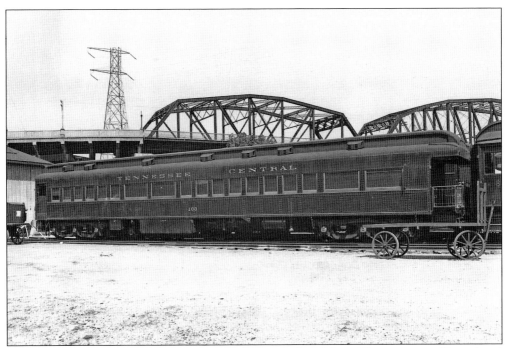

The TC rostered several business cars, such as No. 100 shown here. These were used by railroad executives and their customers while traveling to various cities along the line on business or inspection trips. The open-end observation cars featured additional amenities such as communications equipment, a kitchen, a dining area, and a conference room. These were well-maintained and normally stored behind the Nashville depot. The image below shows a detailed view of the rear brass railing with the distinctive "TC" logo. (Both, Dr. John Payne collection.)

With the rugged terrain as a backdrop, westbound train No. 1 storms across the Emory River shortly after its 12:30 p.m. scheduled departure from Harriman with a four-car consist in tow that included a railway post office, baggage car, and two coaches. In another six hours, the train will safely arrive at TC's riverfront depot in Nashville. (Dr. John Payne collection.)

A special two-car train ascends Brotherton Mountain pulling two cars with the railroad's president and general manager H.W. Stanley in the rear car in 1941. It was routine for the railroad's officers to inspect the right-of-way and property in this manner. This steep grade is one of several along this portion that presented a challenge to crews. (Dr. John Payne collection.)

During the early 1940s at Monterey, train No. 2 has just arrived from Nashville. Judging from the number of automobiles and American flags present at trackside, the occasion is an important one, such as welcoming a returning soldier. The building on the left is the Imperial Hotel. (Monterey Depot Museum.)

Monterey was an active yard for the TC where coal hoppers were assembled into trains and also a servicing point for steam locomotives. In this 1930s scene, train No. 2 has just passed the westbound No. 1 as the flagman prepares to align the switch. (John W. Barriger III photograph, Barriger National Railroad Library, UMSL.)

It is almost departure time as engine No. 551, one of four 4-8-2s built new for the TC by ALCO in 1926, prepares to take passenger train No. 2 out of Nashville on a sunny morning in 1940. The handsome engine will have no problem hauling its three-car train over the steep grades it will encounter on its journey to Harriman. (Dr. John Payne collection.)

In the late 1940s, train No. 2 stops at Emory Gap to discharge passengers. While here, No. 554 will also take on coal and water before continuing on its journey. After trains were dieselized a few years later, the frequent stops for coal and water along the journey were no longer necessary. (Dr. John Payne collection.)

For the small communities along the TC, the passenger train was a vital link to the outside world, and for many, the only transportation option available. On this warm day in the late 1940s, several passengers board train No. 2 at Silver Point, recorded by an unknown passenger aboard the train leaning out the window. (Tennessee State Museum & Archives.)

The house tracks behind the Nashville passenger depot served as the railroad's coach yard, where coaches, business cars, and baggage cars were stored. An unidentified business car is parked next to Railway Express Agency car No. 202. Even years after regular passenger service had been discontinued in 1955, passenger equipment continued to be maintained here for occasional charter trains. (Dr. John Payne collection.)

Train No. 1 is just two miles into its westbound run as it arrives at Emory Gap. The venerable 4-8-2 will require most of the day to ply the remaining 163 miles to reach its Nashville terminus. (Dr. John Payne collection.)

TC locomotive No. 554 prepares to take passenger train No. 2 out of Nashville on a chilly fall morning in 1948. Hours earlier, the overnight westbound train No. 3 had arrived on the adjoining track. Until the discontinuance of the night run in 1949, it was a common sight to see both train sets at the platform at once. (Dr. John Payne collection.)

Revenue from passenger trains comes from a variety of sources. While much of it comes from passenger ticket sales, substantial funds come from two contracting agencies. The US Postal Service operated a railway post office car for the sorting and distribution of mail along the train's route. Another key source of funding was the Railway Express Agency, a company responsible for transporting packages and larger freight to and from various railroad stations across the nation. This 1940s scene shows packages on a wagon that had just been unloaded from TC No. 2 at Crossville. Mail was also handled at most station stops. (Cumberland County Archives and Family Heritage Center collection.)

TC No. 1 has just arrived in Crossville around 1954 with two-year-old ALCO No. 258 on the point, 35 miles into its trip to Nashville. During the brief station stop, freight and express will be loaded and unloaded from the baggage car before the train resumes its westbound journey. (Cumberland County Archives and Family Heritage Center collection.)

The TC had a wide variety of passenger equipment, constructed between 1902 and 1923 by different manufacturers. The last new cars purchased by the company, of all steel construction, went into service in 1923 between Nashville and Harriman. The interior shown here includes plush reclining seats and carpet down the aisle. (Dr. John Payne collection.)

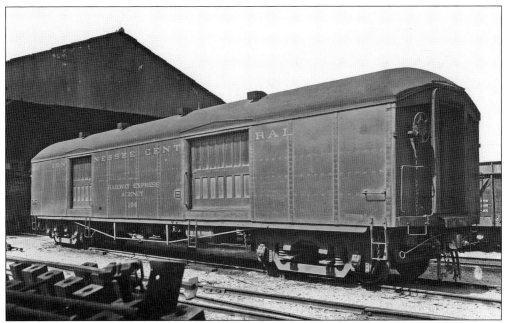

On TC's passenger trains, the Railway Express Agency car was normally the second car in the train set following the railway post office car. These cars hauled express and baggage to the numerous agencies along the route. This car, shown at the car repair shed in Nashville around 1955 after passenger service was discontinued, was later relegated to maintenance-of-way service. (Dr. John Payne collection.)

Few details are known about this photograph. At Monterey, a casket has just been unloaded from the baggage car of TC No. 1, the westbound train to Nashville. The diesel locomotive indicates it was during the early 1950s, perhaps the Korean War period. The honor guard stands at attention as a fallen soldier is carried down the platform and townspeople look on. (Monterey Depot Museum.)

"Tickets, please!" Veteran conductor Pete Mulvihill walks through his train collecting tickets from passengers who had just boarded at the last station. The conductor was the highest ranking crew member on a passenger train and was responsible for keeping both passengers and fellow crew members safe and for maintaining order. Nearly all of the men working for the company had worked there all their lives, as had many of their fathers and perhaps grandfathers. Normally, the conductor would have spent many years in various other positions with the railroad, such as a clerk or laborer, before attaining this respected position. The clerestory roof and mohair "walkover" seats in this picture indicate this coach is older than some of the cars on the trains. (Dr. W.O. Greene III collection.)

During the late afternoon, three cars are spotted at TC's Nashville depot ready to head out the following morning as No. 2 to Harriman. During the overnight layover, the coach will be cleaned and the RPO and baggage car will be loaded. The cars shown here include, from left to right, a railway post office, baggage and express car, and a coach. Below, the following morning, road switcher No. 258 prepares to take the three-car train out of Nashville. Later, the US Postal Service would end its contract with the railroad, ending the operation of the RPO. This led to the discontinuance of the train the following summer. Shelby Street Bridge can be seen in the background below. (Both, Dr. John Payne collection.)

"All aboard!" During a station stop at Lebanon in 1955, the conductor checks his watch and prepares to give the engineer of eastbound No. 2 the highball signal. The scene was recorded by a train passenger from their seat. According to the train bulletin board, the train is due to leave at 9:10 a.m. A few weeks later, on July 31, trains Nos. 1 and 2 were discontinued. The TC had been losing revenue on the lone passenger run for years because of low ridership. Another determining factor was the loss of the RPO car the previous year after it was deemed more efficient to transport mail by a truck than by rail. The depot remained open, serving as a freight office for the TC and the Railway Express Agency. (Both, Wilson County Archives.)

What a treat it must have been to ride a TC train on a warm day with the windows open. This was especially true between Crossville and Rockwood, where trains navigated steep grades, crossed multiple trestles, and entered the railroad's only tunnel. This view, showing the curved Coalbank Hollow Bridge near Rockwood, was snapped by an unknown passenger within a few months of the train's discontinuance in 1955. (Dr. John Payne collection.)

Above, TC's No. 102 was one of several business cars operated by the railroad for inspection trips and special events. It was acquired by the company in the late 1920s from another railroad. To the left is No. 10, the company's only dining car. Below, shop employees check the ice bunkers beneath No. 102 at Nashville in the 1950s before a charter trip. Before modern air conditioning was available, older passenger cars used blocks of ice and fans to help keep car interiors cool. (Above, Dr. John Payne collection; below, G. Battle Claiborne.)

An engineer prepares to couple his locomotive onto a train that had arrived earlier in the day. ALCO switch engine No. 50 has the distinction of being the first diesel locomotive to operate in Nashville. Delivered to the TC in 1939, it remained in service for more than 20 years. (Dr. W.O. Greene III collection.)

While riding on a charter train, the photographer captured this scene from the rear car as it pulled away from the Nashville depot, providing a good view of the station and platform area without cars on any of the tracks. While the passenger station was demolished in 1963, the tracks and platforms continued to be used for excursion trains until the late 1960s. (G. Battle Claiborne.)

Since 1920, the TC operated a dedicated train each summer to Camp Nakanawa in Mayland. Young ladies from various states across the South and Midwest traveled to Nashville, where they boarded a charter train to transport them to the campground near Crossville. After enjoying two months of fresh air, the ladies boarded their train at Mayland for the return trip home. The railroad hosted these annual trips as both a service and as public relations for the company for more than 40 years. On this sunny day, the young ladies make their way toward their preassigned cars before leaving Nashville. A concession car provided soft drinks and snacks during the journey. During the 1950s and 1960s, dressing more formally while traveling was expected—even when going to summer camp. (G. Battle Claiborne.)

At Nashville, young ladies board a TC charter train destined for Camp Nakanawa as their mothers watch to make sure they are safely on board. Because of the unimproved roads in much of the nation during the 1920s and 1930s, getting to the camp by train was the most sensible option. (G. Battle Claiborne.)

Normally, meal service on TC's passenger trains varied from limited to nonexistent. Since the railroad provided no dining car service on the train, an arrangement was made where passengers could order box lunches from the train crew during the trip. During a scheduled stop, the conductor would have the agent call ahead to a Cookeville restaurant where the meals were prepared. When the train arrived in Cookeville, the box lunches were delivered to the hungry passengers. In spite of this arrangement, the railroad did purchase a secondhand car around 1940, converting it into a counter diner. The car was quickly put into service feeding soldiers on troop trains in the mid-1940s. It was also used extensively on charter and excursion trains. When the photograph at left was taken, the diner was providing doughnuts and soft drinks to young ladies on the Camp Nakanawa special. (Both, G. Battle Claiborne.)

Seven

THE 1950s AND DIESELIZATION

The 1950s was a promising era for the railroad industry – a time of renewed growth and modernization. As the decade began, the TC received news that the Tennessee Valley Authority would be building a new coal-fired facility in Roane County, conveniently located near the TC's track near Rockwood. The Kingston Steam Plant would be a major customer receiving thousands of coal hopper cars a year. In anticipation of the large increase in new business, TC's president, H.W. Stanley, applied for and received a $2.25 million loan from the Reconstruction Finance Corporation for purchasing four new locomotives and 200 coal hopper cars and the expansion of rail services that included over seven miles of new spur tracks to serve new mines near Monterey. The new equipment would supply coal to TVA's new steam plant. After the TC acquired its last order of diesel road switchers, it was able to retire its remaining steam locomotives. Passenger traffic on the railroad remained steady during the early 1950s. However, an unexpected decision from the US Postal Service changed the situation. In late 1954, it was announced that the RPO car, the primary way towns along the railroad got their mail, would be removed; it was deemed more efficient to transport mail by truck. Without the RPO, passenger trains were no longer viable financially. Effective that November, train Nos. 1 and 2 were without mail service, guaranteeing they would not survive much longer. The TC discontinued its last passenger train on July 31, 1955. By the middle of the decade, the future of the Road of Personal Service was not looking as promising as it had been a few years earlier. The TVA began to purchase more of its coal from mines located along the Louisville & Nashville Railroad. Elsewhere on the TC, as on other railroads, more and more freight was moving by truck as highways, such as the parallel US Route 70, were widened and improved. It was a trend that could not be reversed.

Between 1951 and 1956, the railroad purchased several class RS-3 locomotives from ALCO, the "RS" signifying road switcher. These first-generation diesels were intended as replacements for the last of the steam power. TC No. 259, one of the last of these models built for the railroad, is seen on the turntable at the Nashville yard while being serviced between runs. The RS-3s proved to be real workhorses for the railroad. On longer freight trains, they were often coupled to the more streamlined ALCO FA-1, providing additional power for getting over steeper grades. (James D. Le Croy.)

In the 1950s, Hi-Rail vehicles were becoming a common sight on many of the larger railroads. For smaller lines such as the TC, they were an unusual find. A Hi-Rail can operate on both highways and railroad tracks. In addition to regular wheels with tires, Hi-Rail vehicles also have a set of flanged steel wheels that, when deployed, allow them to travel safely on rails. The car shown here at the Nashville Shops is a 1955 Pontiac four-door wagon, probably the only type owned by the TC at the time. The retracted wheels are visible at front and rear. The customized bumpers protruded to allow room to store the flanged wheels. The additional marker lights provided added visibility. (G. Battle Claiborne.)

TC road switcher No. 256 and a caboose pose for a photographer at Monterey between assignments during the 1950s. Monterey was an active place on the railroad and contained servicing facilities that once included a roundhouse, water tank, and coal tower. At this yard, cars loaded with coal from mines on the Crawford branch were added to trains. (Monterey Depot Museum.)

In 1952, the Reconstruction Finance Corporation approved a $2.25 million loan to TC for the purchase of four new diesel locomotives from ALCO and 200 coal hopper cars from the Pullman-Standard Company. These were needed to transport coal to the Tennessee Valley Authority's new Kingston steam plant. Hopper No. 9699 was one of those cars. (Pullman-Standard Company photograph, Dr. W.O. Greene III collection.)

An eastbound freight, led by an FA-1 class locomotive, slowly heads along the curvy track hugging the Tennessee hills along the bank of the Caney Fork River near Lancaster. This vista has changed little since this photograph was taken in the 1950s. (J. Parker Lamb, Collection of the Center for Railroad Photography & Art.)

A TC employee adds sand to No.801 at the Nashville yard under the watchful eye of the locomotive's engineer. The railroad purchased five FA-1 units from ALCO in 1949 to power both passenger and freight trains. This locomotive remained in service for 18 years before being scrapped. (J. Parker Lamb, Collection of the Center for Railroad Photography & Art.)

The Highballer

TENNESSEE CENTRAL RAILWAY
The Road of  Personal Service

VOLUME I – JANUARY–FEBRUARY–1956–NO. I

At the suggestion of several employees, the TC began publishing its first company magazine in early 1956. The name was chosen in a vote by employees. The magazine, which was published every other month, covered the "goings-on" over the entire railroad. Much of the emphasis was on employees and their families, specifically weddings, births, retirements, and deaths. The balance of the content covered company news such as the delivery of new locomotives, rolling stock, or the addition of new industries along the line and the communities the railroad served. The cover of the first issue featured a posed photograph of a freight train with an ALCO FA and booster unit near the tunnel under Mount Roosevelt, west of Rockwood. In spite of its popularity, *The Highballer* was only printed for a couple of years before ceasing publication. (Author's collection.)

Nashville's Bryan River and Rail Terminal was the only true transloading location on the TC. The facility, which opened in 1922, was initially owned and managed by the city. However, by the 1950s, Bryan Terminal was losing money and various companies were contracted to operate it at a profit. In later years, much of the terminal was leased out for warehouse space. In this scene, terminal employees load freight into boxcars as a crane in the background lifts another pallet from a barge docked on the adjoining Cumberland River. Once loaded, the freight cars were moved to the TC's main yard to wait for the next available train. (Metro Nashville Archives, Banner Negatives collection.)

During most of the TC's history, it favored locomotives built by ALCO. Beginning with the popular 2-8-0 models in 1902, the railroad purchased both new and used motive power from ALCO. The company's brand loyalty continued into the era of dieselization. In 1939, the TC purchased its first diesel locomotive, No. 50, for use in switching cars in its yard. Ten years later, the railroad began regularly ordering diesels from ALCO when it ordered five FA-1 units and an FB-1 booster for powering its passenger and freight trains as a replacement for the steam locomotives being retired. In this portrait, one of the locomotives, fresh from the paint booth, sports the iconic flat nose and ALCO–General Electric grill around the headlight that gave this model its unique look. (Author's collection.)

In anticipation of an increase in traffic, the TC acquired additional motive power and rolling stock. Covered hopper No. 6000 was the first of 10 such cars purchased from the Greenville Steel Car Company. In the years to come, the TC struggled to pay off the loans for this equipment. These photographs were taken by the manufacturer at its Pennsylvania plant before the cars were delivered to the railroad in 1957. (Both, Greenville Steel Company, Dr. W.O. Greene III collection.)

Between assignments, locomotives are refueled and thoroughly checked for safe operation before heading out on the next train. A yard man stands carefully on the hood as he adds sand to engine No. 259 in Nashville. When operating a train, the engineer applies sand as necessary to improve traction when the locomotive's wheels start to slip on wet or oily tracks and steep grades. This locomotive was one of 13 ALCO RS-3 models purchased by the TC in the 1950s. (James D. Le Croy.)

Several of the train crew enjoy a fall day while riding on the platform of their locomotive as it pulls a westbound local over a trestle near Clarksville. Over the decades, the many wooden trestles along the TC became a maintenance nightmare for the railroad. (J. Parker Lamb, Collection of the Center for Railroad Photography & Art.)

On the morning of April 9, 1957, TC freight train No. 84 departed Nashville's yard at 4:40 a.m. with a crew of five, destined for Harriman. At approximately 5:45 a.m., as the eastbound 58-car train was passing through the Martha community, the engineer sounded his horn for the highway crossing at US Route 70 North. A tractor-trailer suddenly appeared, approaching at high speed, and rammed the side of the lead locomotive. The tremendous impact derailed all three locomotives as well as the first 14 cars of the train. The crewmen of the train sustained minor injuries; however, the driver of the truck was killed instantly. Since it was daylight and both warning bells and lights were working properly, there was no explanation of why the heavily loaded truck did not stop. Fortunately, the train's six tank cars containing butane and high octane gasoline, although punctured, did not explode. The track was restored to full service the following afternoon. This view shows the lead unit at far right turned in the opposite direction. (Neal Blackburn.)

Employees at TC's Summit yard near Clarksville move quickly to get a Nashville, Chattanooga & St. Louis Railway gondola back on the track after a derailment left several freight cars on the ground on the TC's Western Division between Nashville and Hopkinsville. Every moment a disabled car remains on an active track means long delays for other trains. From an occupational safety aspect, this scene is in stark contrast to how workers today would respond to a similar wreck. Today's crew would have safety hats, goggles, and reflective vests. These men had none of that. To them, it was just another day on the job. (Dr. John Payne collection.)

Two locomotives carry a freight train over the Southern Railway line near Harriman on the far eastern end of the TC. Between Harriman and Crossville, the railroad navigated the most rugged terrain on the system, spanning numerous tall trestles over several railroad tracks, industrial spurs leading to trackside industries, as well as various rivers and ravines. (James D. Le Croy collection.)

A westbound TC freight rumbles across a bridge over the Louisville & Nashville Railroad's Memphis to Bowling Green, Kentucky, line as locomotive No. 260 brings a long freight train into Clarksville on a lazy summer day. After doing some switching of cars, the train will continue to its final destination at Hopkinsville. (J. Parker Lamb, Collection of the Center for Railroad Photography & Art.)

The photographer captured this scene moments after the photograph on the previous page at the same Clarksville location. In this classic train-over-train picture, a northbound Louisville & Nashville train traveling north on the road's Memphis line prepares to duck under the Western Division of the TC as the caboose of a westbound local train passes. This was one of five locations in middle Tennessee where the L&N and TC crossed. (J. Parker Lamb, Collection of the Center for Railroad Photography & Art.)

Over the years, the TC collected an interesting variety of equipment and rolling stock. Many of the older cars remained on the property well past their useful life. These cars were often downgraded to maintenance-of-way service, storage space, or whatever purposes best suited the railroad. At the time this picture was taken, this deteriorated vintage car, numbered W2000, was at the Nashville Shops parked near the car repair shed. Built in the late 1890s, this open-vestibule car was at one point used in regular passenger service on another railroad. Reportedly, TC purchased the car from a private owner during the 1940s and relegated it to maintenance-of-way and wreck train service through the 1950s. (James D. Le Croy.)

BIBLIOGRAPHY

The Highballer, 1956–1958.

Nashville American, *Nashville Banner*, and *Nashville Tennessean* newspapers, 1895–1955.

Official Railway Guide, 1895–1939.

Sulzer, Elmer G. *Ghost Railroads of Tennessee*. Indianapolis, IN: Vane A. Jones Company, 1975.

Tennessee Central Railway company records, 1884–1968.

DISCOVER THOUSANDS OF LOCAL HISTORY BOOKS FEATURING MILLIONS OF VINTAGE IMAGES

Arcadia Publishing, the leading local history publisher in the United States, is committed to making history accessible and meaningful through publishing books that celebrate and preserve the heritage of America's people and places.

Find more books like this at
www.arcadiapublishing.com

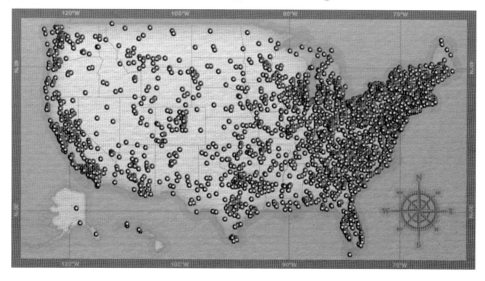

Search for your hometown history, your old stomping grounds, and even your favorite sports team.